may you be full

Reclaimed Joy Journal

By Lisa Jennings

Shout with joy to the Lord, all the earth!
Worship the Lord with gladness.
Come before him, singing with joy.
Acknowledge that the Lord is God!
He made us, and we are his.
We are his people, the sheep of his pasture.
Enter his gates with thanksgiving;
go into his courts with praise.
Give thanks to him and praise his name.
For the Lord is good.
His unfailing love continues forever,
and his faithfulness continues to each generation.

Psalm 100 (TPT)

Reclaimed Joy Journal
© 2022 by Lisa Jennings

Published with help from 100X Publishing
Olympia, Washington | www.100Xacademy.com

All rights reserved. No part of this publication may be reproduced, stored in a retrieval system, or transmitted in any form or by any means--for example, electronic, photocopy, recording--without the prior written permission of the publisher.
Holy Bible, New International Version®, NIV®: Copyright ©1973, 1978, 1984, 2011 by Biblica, Inc.® Used by permission. All rights reserved worldwide.
NET Bible® copyright ©1996-2017 by Biblical Studies Press, L.L.C. http://netbible.com All rights reserved.
The Living Bible copyright © 1971 by Tyndale House Foundation. Used by permission of Tyndale House Publishers Inc., Carol Stream, Illinois 60188. All rights reserved.
Amplified Bible, Classic Edition (AMPC): Copyright © 1954, 1958, 1962, 1964, 1965, 1987 by The Lockman Foundation.
The Passion Translation® (TPT). Copyright © 2017, 2018, 2020 by Passion & Fire Ministries, Inc. Used by permission. All rights reserved. thePassionTranslation.com.
The Message (MSG): Copyright © 1993, 2002, 2018 by Eugene H. Peterson.
GOD'S WORD Translation (GW): Copyright © 1995, 2003, 2013, 2014, 2019, 2020 by God's Word to the Nations Mission Society. All rights reserved.

This *Reclaimed Joy Journal* was created to be a companion on your journey to discovering ways to reclaim your joy. Whether it's being used alongside the book *Reclaimed Joy: Discovering the God of Wonders in Your Whys* or by itself, it will aide you to draw from the deep wells of life and freedom the Lord longs to give to you.

For over 35 years, my heart has moved my pen to page, journaling my feelings, God's wisdom and revelations that come. Through times of reflection, I have found deeper understanding of God and myself.

If you choose to couple this journal with the *Reclaimed Joy* book, it features ten verses from each chapter with lines for writing. There is also one quote from each chapter to separate them. Each page unveils the beautiful reminder of God's goodness towards us.

Though this journal has a lovely rhythm to flow with the book, it is not necessary to have the book to use it. My heart is for you to spend time with God in a way that fits your needs and personality. My prayer for your journaling time is:

"Joyfully you will draw from the springs of deliverance."
Isaiah 12:3 NET Bible

"Your lives light up the world. Let others see your light from a distance, for how can you hide a city that stands on a hilltop?

And who would light a lamp and then hide it in an obscure place? Instead, it's placed where everyone in the house can benefit from its light.

So don't hide your light! Let it shine brightly before others, so that the commendable things you do will shine as light upon them, and then they will give their praise to your Father in heaven."

Matthew 5:14-16 (TPT)

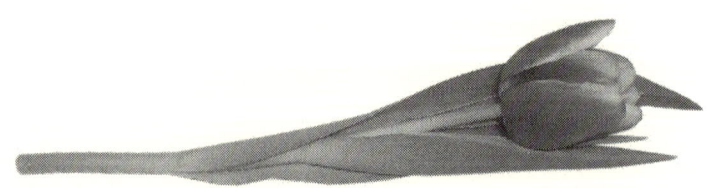

> *"Lord, you delivered me safely from my mother's womb. You are the one who cared for me ever since I was a baby. Since the day I was born, I've been placed in your custody. You've cradled me throughout my days. I've trusted and you've always been my God."*
>
> Psalm 22:9-10 (TPT)

_____
_____
_____
_____
_____
_____
_____
_____
_____
_____
_____
_____
_____
_____
_____
_____
_____
_____
_____
_____
_____
_____
_____
_____
_____
_____
_____

"Thank you for responding to me; you've truly become my salvation! This is God's work. We rub our eyes we can hardly believe it!"

Psalm 118: 21 The Message (paraphrased)

_____
_____
_____
_____
_____
_____
_____
_____
_____
_____
_____
_____
_____
_____
_____
_____
_____
_____
_____
_____
_____
_____
_____
_____
_____
_____
_____
_____

"This is the very day God acted let's celebrate and be festive! Salvation now, God. Salvation now! Oh yes, God—a free and full life!"

Psalm 118:23-24 The Message

> "I'll call nobodies and make them somebodies; I'll call the unloved and make them beloved. In the place where they yelled out, 'You're nobody!' they're calling you 'God's living children.'"
>
> Romans 9:25-26 The Message

"Tell me where you want me to go and I will go there. May every fiber of my being unite in reverence to your name."

Psalm 86:11 TLB

My deep need calls to the deep kindness of your love. Your waterfall of weeping sent waves of sorrow over my soul, carrying me away, cascading over me like a thundering cataract.

Psalm 42:7 TPT

"For to us a Child is born, to us a Son is given; and the government shall be upon His shoulder, and His name shall be called Wonderful Counselor, Mighty God, Everlasting Father [of Eternity], Prince of Peace..."

Isaiah 9:6 (AMPC)

"For just one day of intimacy with you is like a thousand days of joy rolled into one! I'd rather stand at the threshold in front of the Gate Beautiful, ready to go in and worship my God, than to live my life without you in the most beautiful palace of the wicked."

Psalm 84:10 TPT

> *"I am standing in absolute stillness, silent before the one I love, waiting as long as it takes for him to rescue me. Only God is my Savior, and he will not fail me."*
>
> Psalm 62:5 TPT

> "Never doubt God's mighty power to work in you and accomplish all this. He will achieve infinitely more than your greatest request, your most unbelievable dream, and exceed your wildest imagination! He will outdo them all, for his miraculous power constantly energizes you."
>
> Ephesians 3:20 TPT

"Yes, furthermore, I count everything as loss compared to the possession of the priceless privilege (the overwhelming preciousness, the surpassing worth, and supreme advantage) of knowing Christ Jesus my Lord and of progressively becoming more deeply and intimately acquainted with Him [of perceiving and recognizing and understanding Him more fully and clearly].

For His sake I have lost everything and consider it all to be mere rubbish (refuse, dregs), in order that I may win (gain) Christ (the Anointed One)."

Philippians 3:8 AMPC

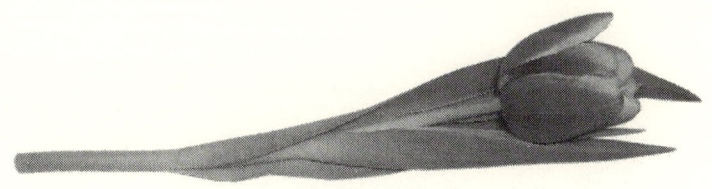

For the Lord is a God of justice. Blessed (happy, fortunate, to be envied) are all those who [earnestly] wait for Him, who expect and look and long for Him [for His victory, His favor, His love, His peace, His joy, and His matchless, unbroken companionship].

Isaiah 30:18 AMPC (paraphrased)

_____
_____
_____
_____
_____
_____
_____
_____
_____
_____
_____
_____
_____
_____
_____
_____
_____
_____
_____
_____
_____
_____
_____
_____

"Heaven is My throne and the earth my footstool..."
Isaiah 66:1 AMPC

"I call to you, God, because I'm sure of an answer. So—answer! Bend our ear! listen sharp! Paint grace-graffiti on the fences; take in your frightened children who are running from the neighborhood bullies straight to you."

Psalm 17:6-7 The Message

"Let me escape from these cruel and wicked men, and save me from the hands of the evil one. For you are my only hope, Lord! I've hung on to you, trusting in you all my life."

Psalm 71:4-5 TPT

"It was you who supported me from the day I was born, loving me, helping me through my life's journey. You've made me into a miracle; no wonder I trust you and praise you forever! Many marvel at my success, but I know it is all because of you, my mighty protector! I'm overflowing with your praise for all you've done, and your splendor thrills me all day long."

Psalm 71:6-8 TPT

"And everything I've taught you is so that the peace which is in me will be in you and will give you great confidence as you rest in me. For in this unbelieving world you will experience trouble and sorrows, but you must be courageous, for I have conquered the world!"

John 16:33 TPT

"Wherever I go, your hand will guide me, your strength will empower me."

Psalm 139:10 TPT

> "A broken reed He will not break [off] And a dimly burning wick He will not extinguish [He will not harm those who are weak and suffering]; He will faithfully bring forth justice."
>
> Isaiah 42:3 AMP

Yet God is the God of harmony, not confusion or instability.
1 Corinthians 14:33 TPT (paraphrased)

> *"I don't depend on my own strength to accomplish this; however I do have one compelling focus: I forget all of the past as I fasten my heart to the future instead."*
>
> Philippians 3:13 TPT

"It's impossible to disappear from you or to ask the darkness to hide me, for your presence is everywhere, bringing light into my night."

Psalms 139:11 TPT

> *"He won't brush aside the bruised and the hurt and he won't disregard the small and insignificant, but he'll steadily and firmly set things right. He won't tire out and quit. He won't be stopped until he's finished his work—to set things right on earth..."*
>
> Isaiah 42:3 The Message

"But the Comforter (Counselor, Helper, Intercessor, Advocate, Strengthener, Standby), the Holy Spirit, Whom the Father will send in My name [in My place, to represent Me and act on My behalf], He will teach you all things. And He will cause you to recall (will remind you of, bring to your remembrance) everything I have told you."

John 14:26 AMPC

_____
_____
_____
_____
_____
_____
_____
_____
_____
_____
_____
_____
_____
_____
_____
_____
_____
_____
_____
_____
_____
_____
_____
_____
_____

> *"As far as the east is from the west, so far has He removed our transgressions from us."*
>
> Psalms 103:12 AMPC

> "Your words were found, and I ate them; and Your words were to me a joy and the rejoicing of my heart, for I am called by Your name, O Lord God of hosts."
>
> Jeremiah 15:16 AMPC

"Behold You desire truth in the inner being: make me therefore to know wisdom in my inmost heart."

Psalm 51:6 AMPC

_____
_____
_____
_____
_____
_____
_____
_____
_____
_____
_____
_____
_____
_____
_____
_____
_____
_____
_____
_____
_____
_____
_____
_____
_____
_____
_____
_____
_____

> *"But the moment one turns to the Lord with an open heart, the veil is lifted and they see. Now, the 'Lord' I'm referring to is the Holy Spirit, and wherever he is Lord, there is freedom."*
>
> 2 Corinthians 3:16-17 TPT

> *"He is the atoning sacrifice for our sins, and not only ours but also the sins of the whole world."*
>
> 1 John 2:2 TPT

"Learn this well: unless you receive the revelation of the kingdom the same way a little child receives it, you will never be able to enter in."
Luke 18:17 TPT

_____
_____
_____
_____
_____
_____
_____
_____
_____
_____
_____
_____
_____
_____
_____
_____
_____
_____
_____
_____
_____
_____
_____
_____
_____
_____
_____
_____
_____

"Store it in your heart, speak it out loud, use it as a prayer. "Your word have I laid up in my heart that I might not sin against you.""

Psalm 119:11 AMPC

> "God is not a man, that He should tell or act a lie, neither the son of man, that He should feel repentance or compunction [for what He has promised]. Has He said and shall He not do it? Or has He spoken and shall He not make it good?"
>
> Numbers 23:19 AMPC

"Real isn't how you are made," said the Skin Horse. "It's a thing that happens to you. When a child loves you for a long, long time, not just to play with, but REALLY loves you, then you become Real."

"Does it hurt?" asked the Rabbit.

"Sometimes," said the Skin Horse, for he was always truthful. "When you are Real you don't mind being hurt."

"Does it happen all at once, like being wound up," he asked, "or bit by bit?"

"It doesn't happen all at once," said the Skin Horse. "You become. It takes a long time. That's why it doesn't happen often to people who break easily, or have sharp edges, or who have to be carefully kept. Generally, by the time you are Real, most of your hair has been loved off, and your eyes drop out and you get loose in the joints and very shabby. But these things don't matter at all, because once you are Real you can't be ugly, except to people who don't understand."

—The Velveteen Rabbit

"Surely He has borne our griefs (sicknesses, weaknesses, and distresses) and carried our sorrows and pains [of punishment], yet we [ignorantly] considered Him stricken, smitten, and afflicted by God [as if with leprosy]. But He was wounded for our transgressions, He was bruised for our guilt and iniquities; the chastisement [needful to obtain] peace and well-being for us was upon Him, and with the stripes [that wounded] Him we are healed and made whole."

Isaiah 53:4-5 AMPC

"God shows no partiality undue favor or unfairness; with Him one man is not different from another."

Romans 2:11 AMPC

"There is no room in love for fear. Well-formed love banishes fear. Since fear is crippling, a fearful life—fear of death, fear of judgment—is one not yet fully formed in love."

1 John 4:18 The Message

"...keep your thoughts continually fixed on all that is authentic and real, honorable and admirable, beautiful and respectful, pure and holy, merciful and kind. And fasten your thoughts on every glorious work of God, praising him always."

Philippians 4:8 TPT

_____
_____
_____
_____
_____
_____
_____
_____
_____
_____
_____
_____
_____
_____
_____
_____
_____
_____
_____
_____
_____
_____
_____

"Joyful is the person who finds wisdom, the one who gains understanding. For wisdom is more profitable than silver, and her wages are better than gold. Wisdom is more precious than rubies, nothing you desire can compare with her. She offers you long life in her right hand, and riches and honor in her left, She will guide you down delightful paths; all her ways are satisfying. Wisdom is a tree of life to those who embrace her; happy are those who hold her tightly."

Proverbs 3:13 NLT

_____
_____
_____
_____
_____
_____
_____
_____
_____
_____
_____
_____
_____
_____
_____
_____
_____
_____
_____
_____
_____

"And God-Enthroned spoke to me and said, "Consider this! I am making everything to be new and fresh. Write down at once all that I have told you, because each word is trustworthy and dependable."

Revelation 21:5 TPT

"Behold, at that time I will deal with all those who afflict you; I will save the limping [ones] and gather the outcasts and will make them a praise and a name in every land of their shame."

Zephaniah 3:19 AMPC

"At that time I will bring you in; yes, at that time I will gather you, for I will make you a name and a praise among all the nations of the earth when I reverse your captivity before your eyes, says the Lord."

Zephaniah 3:20 AMPC

"For we have the living Word of God, which is full of energy, and it pierces more sharply than a two-edged sword. It will even penetrate to the very core of our being where soul and spirit, bone and marrow meet. It interprets and reveals the true thoughts and secret motives of our hearts."

Hebrews 4:12 TPT

_____
_____
_____
_____
_____
_____
_____
_____
_____
_____
_____
_____
_____
_____
_____
_____
_____
_____
_____
_____
_____
_____
_____

> *"...for tremendous power is released through the passionate, heartfelt prayer of a godly believer!"*
>
> James 5:16 TPT

*"There is nothing more rare, nor more beautiful, than a woman being apologetically herself; comfortable in her perfect imperfection.
To me, that is the true essence of beauty."*

—Steve Maraboli

> *"We have this certain hope like a strong, unbreakable anchor holding our souls to God himself. Our anchor of hope is fastened to the mercy seat which sits in the heavenly realm beyond the sacred threshold."*
>
> Hebrews 6:19 TPT

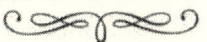

"For the vision is yet for an appointed time and it hastens to the end [fulfillment]; it will not deceive or disappoint. Though it tarry, wait [earnestly] for it, because it will surely come; it will not be behindhand on its appointed day."

Habakkuk 2:3 AMPC

"And God spoke to Israel in visions of the night and said, 'Jacob, Jacob." And He said, 'Here I am.'"

Genesis 46:2 ESV

> *"In that way, whatever happens to one member happens to all. If one suffers, everyone suffers. If one is honored, everyone rejoices."*
>
> 1 Corinthians 12:26 TPT

"The one I love calls to me: Arise, my dearest. Hurry, my darling. Come away with me! I have come as you have asked to draw you to my heart and lead you out. For now is the time, my beautiful one."

Song Of Songs 2:10 TPT

> *"The season has changed, the bondage of your barren winter has ended and the season of hiding is over and gone. The rains have soaked the earth..."*
>
> Song Of Songs 2:11 TPT

"...and left it bright with blossoming flowers. The season for singing and pruning the vines has arrived. I hear the cooing of doves in our land, filling the air with songs to awaken you and guide you forth."

Song Of Songs 2:12 TPT

"Can you not discern this new day of destiny breaking forth around you? The early signs of my purposes and plans are bursting forth. The budding vines of new life are now blooming everywhere."

Song Of Songs 2:13 TPT

> "The fragrance of their flowers whispers, 'There is change in the air.' Arise, my love, my beautiful companion, and run with me to the higher place. For now is the time to arise and come away with me."
>
> Song Of Songs 2:13 continued TPT

> *"Listen, my dearest darling, you are so beautiful—
> you are beauty itself to me!"*
>
> Song Of Songs 4:1 TPT

"GOD, my shepherd! I don't need a thing.

You have bedded me down in lush meadows, you find me quiet pools to drink from.

True to your word, you let me catch my breath and send me in the right direction."

Psalm 23:1-3 The Message

"Oh! May the God of green hope fill you up with joy, fill you up with peace, so that your believing lives, filled with the life-giving energy of the Holy Spirit, will brim over with hope!"

Romans 15:13 The Message

"Celebrate with those who celebrate, and weep with those who grieve."

Romans 12:15 TPT

"Live happily together in a spirit of harmony, and be as mindful of another's worth as you are your own. Don't live with a lofty mind-set, thinking you are too important to serve others, but be willing to do menial tasks and identify with those who are humble minded. Don't be smug or even think for a moment that you know it all."

Romans 12:16 TPT

"The revelation of God is whole and pulls our lives together. The signposts of God are clear and point out the right road. The life-maps of God are right, showing the way to joy. The directions of God are plain and easy on the eyes. God's reputation is twenty-four-carat gold, with a lifetime guarantee. The decisions of God are accurate down to the nth degree."

Psalm 19:7-9 The Message

> *"Humble yourselves, therefore, under God's mighty hand, that he may lift you up in due time."*
>
> 1 Peter 5:6 NIV

"Yes, you are my darling companion. You stand out from all the rest. For the curse of sin surround you, still you remain as pure as a lily, even more than all the others."

Song of Songs 2:2 TPT

_____
_____
_____
_____
_____
_____
_____
_____
_____
_____
_____
_____
_____
_____
_____
_____
_____
_____
_____
_____
_____
_____
_____
_____
_____
_____
_____

"Love the Lord your God with every passion of your heart, with all the energy of your being, and with every thought that is within you.' This is the great and supreme commandment. And the second is like it in importance: 'You must love your friend in the same way you love yourself.'"

Matthew 22:37-39 TPT

> *"I'm obviously not trying to flatter you or water down my message to be popular with men, but my supreme passion is to please God. For if all I attempt to do is please people, I would not be the true servant of the Messiah."*
>
> Galatians 1:10 TPT

> "Let everyone be devoted to fulfill the work God has given them to do with excellence, and their joy will be in doing what's right and being themselves, and not in being affirmed by others. Every believer is ultimately responsible for his or her own conscience."
>
> Galatians 6:4-5 TPT

> *"God's marvelous grace imparts to each one of us varying gifts and ministries that are uniquely ours..."*
>
> Romans 12:6 TPT

"Nothing and no one can resist God's Word. We can't get away from it—no matter what. Now that we know what we have—Jesus, this great High Priest with ready access to God—let's not let it slip through our fingers. We don't have a priest who is out of touch with our reality. He's been through weakness and testing, experienced it all—all but the sin. So let's walk right up to him and get what he is so ready to give. Take the mercy, accept the help."

Hebrews 4:13-16 The Message

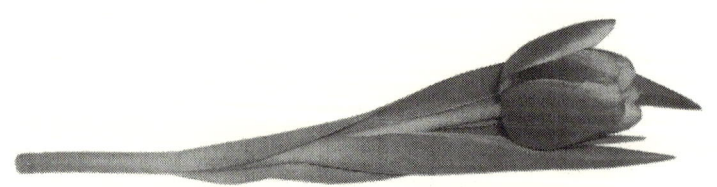

> *"But God shows his love for us that while we were still sinners, Christ died for us."*
>
> Romans 5:8 ESV

> *"And God saw everything that He had made, and behold, it was very good (suitable, pleasant) and He approved it completely. And there was evening and there was morning, a sixth day"*
>
> Genesis 1:31 AMPC

> *"For 'the serpent was more subtle and crafty than any living creature of the field which the Lord God had made...'"*
>
> Genesis 3:1 AMPC

"He has made everything beautiful in its time."
Ecclesiastes 3:11 NIV

You will guard me and keep me in perfect and constant peace whose mind [both its inclination and its character] is stayed on You, because I commit myself to You, lean on You, and hope confidently in You. So trust in the Lord (commit yourself to Him, lean on Him, hope confidently in Him) forever; for the Lord God is an everlasting Rock [the Rock of Ages].

Isaiah 26:3-4 AMPC (paraphrased)

"Lord, You will ordain peace (God's favor and blessings, both temporal and spiritual) for us, for You have also wrought in us and for us all our work."

Isaiah 26:12 AMPC

"Put on God's whole armor [the armor of a heavy-armed soldier which God supplies], that you may be able successfully to stand up against [all] the strategies and the deceits of the devil. For we are not wrestling with flesh and blood [contending only with physical opponents], but against the despotisms, against the powers, against [the master spirits who are] the world rulers of this present darkness, against the spirit forces of wickedness in the heavenly (supernatural) sphere."

Ephesians 6:11 AMPC

_____
_____
_____
_____
_____
_____
_____
_____
_____
_____
_____
_____
_____
_____
_____
_____
_____
_____
_____
_____
_____
_____

"The promise of 'arrival' and 'rest' is still there for God's people."
Hebrews 4:9 The Message

"Be free from pride-filled opinions, for they will only harm your cherished unity. Don't allow self-promotion to hide in your hearts, but in authentic humility put others first and view others as more important than yourselves. Abandon every display of selfishness. Possess a greater concern for what matters to others instead of your own interests. And consider the example that Jesus, the Anointed One, has set before us. Let his mindset become your motivation."

Philippians 2:3-5 TPT

"Shake yourself from the dust; arise, sit [erect in a dignified place], O Jerusalem; loose yourself from the bonds of your neck, O captive Daughter of Zion."

Isaiah 52:2 AMPC

"We serve a good and merciful God who promises to bring beauty from the ashes regardless if we are the ones who lit the match and fanned the flames, blowing into it or not."

–Lisa Jennings

> *"Fear not, for you shall not be ashamed; neither be confounded and depressed, for you shall not be put to shame. For you shall forget the shame of your youth..."*
>
> Isaiah 54:4 AMPC

"...now salvation and power are set in place, and the kingdom reign of our God and the ruling authority of his Anointed One are established. For the accuser of our brothers and sisters, who relentlessly accused them day and night before our God, has now been defeated—cast out once and for all. They conquered him completely through the blood of the Lamb and the powerful word of his testimony..."

Revelation 12:10-11 TPT

"And the ransomed of the Lord shall return, and come to Zion with songs and everlasting joy upon their heads: they shall obtain joy and gladness and sorrow and sighing shall flee away..."

Isaiah 35:10 **KJV**

"To show that you are the children of your Father Who is in heaven; for He makes the sun to rise on the wicked and the good, and makes the rain fall upon the upright and the wrongdoers alike."

Matthew 5:45 AMPC

"'There are many valiant and noble ones, but you have ascended above them all!' Charm can be misleading, and beauty is vain and so quickly fades, but this virtuous woman lives in the wonder, awe, and fear of the Lord. She will be praised throughout eternity. So go ahead and give her the credit that is due, for she has become a radiant woman and all her loving works of righteousness deserve to be admired at the gateways of every city!"

Proverbs 31:29-31 TPT

"The wilderness and the dry land shall be glad; the desert shall rejoice and blossom like the rose and the autumn crocus."

Isaiah 35:1 AMPC

"So Jesus went over it again, 'I speak to you eternal truth: I am the Gate for the flock. All those who broke in before me are thieves who came to steal, but the sheep never listened to them. I am the Gateway. To enter through me is to experience life, freedom, and satisfaction.'"

John 10:7-9 TPT

"A thief has only one thing in mind—he wants to steal, slaughter, and destroy. But I have come to give you everything in abundance, more than you expect—life in its fullness until you overflow."

John 10:10 TPT

_____
_____
_____
_____
_____
_____
_____
_____
_____
_____
_____
_____
_____
_____
_____
_____
_____
_____
_____
_____
_____
_____
_____
_____
_____
_____
_____
_____

"He has brought me to his banqueting place, and his banner over me is love [waving overhead to protect and comfort me]."

Song of Solomon 2:4 AMPC

> "You empower me for victory with your wrap-around presence. Your power within makes me strong to subdue, and by stooping down in gentleness you strengthened me and made me great! You've set me free from captivity and now I'm standing complete, ready to fight some more!"
>
> Psalm 18:35-36 TPT

"GOD makes everything come out right; he puts victims back on their feet. He showed Moses how he went about his work, opened up his plans to all Israel.

GOD is sheer mercy and grace; not easily angered, he's rich in love. He doesn't endlessly nag and scold, nor hold grudges forever. He doesn't treat us as our sins deserve, nor pay us back in full for our wrongs.

As high as heaven is over the earth, so strong is his love to those who fear him."

Psalm 103:6-18 The Message

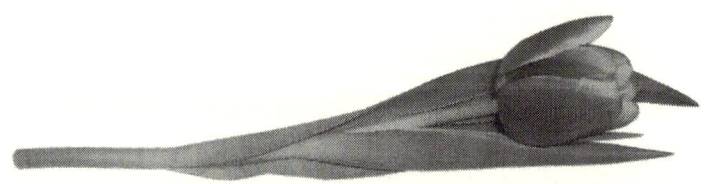

"But Lord, your endless love stretches from one eternity to the other, unbroken and unrelenting toward those who fear you and those who bow face down in awe before you. Your faithfulness to keep every gracious promise you've made passes from parents, to children, to grandchildren, and beyond."

Psalms 103:17 TPT

> *"Ask, and the gift is yours. Seek, and you'll discover. Knock, and the door will be opened for you. For every persistent one will get what he asks for. Every persistent seeker will discover what he longs for. And everyone who knocks persistently will one day find an open door."*
>
> Matthew 7:7-8 TPT

_____
_____
_____
_____
_____
_____
_____
_____
_____
_____
_____
_____
_____
_____
_____
_____
_____
_____
_____
_____
_____
_____
_____
_____
_____
_____

> "And I will give you a new heart, and I will put a new spirit in you. I will take out your stony, stubborn heart and give you a tender, responsive heart."
>
> Ezekiel 36:26 NLT

> *"But instead be kind and affectionate toward one another. Has God graciously forgiven you? Then graciously forgive one another in the depths of Christ's love..."*
>
> Ephesians 4:32 TPT

> *"Lay aside bitter words, temper tantrums, revenge, profanity, and insults."*
>
> Ephesians 4:31 TPT

"Stay away from anger and revenge. Keep envy far from you, for it only leads you into lies."

Psalm 37:8 TPT

"...chasing after things instead of God, manipulating others, hatred of those who get in your way, senseless arguments, resentment when others are favored, temper tantrums, angry quarrels, only thinking of yourself, being in love with your own opinions..."

Galatians 5:20 TPT

_____
_____
_____
_____
_____
_____
_____
_____
_____
_____
_____
_____
_____
_____
_____
_____
_____
_____
_____
_____
_____
_____
_____
_____
_____

"Never hold a grudge or try to get even, but plan your life around the noblest way to benefit others. Do your best to live as everybody's friend."
Romans 12:17-18 TPT

> "Beloved, don't be obsessed with taking revenge, but leave that to God's righteous justice. For the Scriptures say: 'Vengeance is mine, and I will repay,' says the Lord."
>
> Romans 12:19 TPT

> *"Later Peter approached Jesus and said, 'How many times do I have to forgive my fellow believer who keeps offending me? Seven times?' Jesus answered, 'Not seven times, Peter, but seventy times seven times!'"*
>
> Matthew 18:21-22 TPT

"Everything we could ever need for life and complete devotion to God has already been deposited in us by his divine power. For all this was lavished upon us through the rich experience of knowing him who has called us by name and invited us to come to him through a glorious manifestation of his goodness..."

2 Peter 1:3 TPT

"'For I know the plans I have for you,' declares the Lord, 'plans to prosper you and not to harm you, plans to give you hope and a future.'"

Jeremiah 29:11 NIV

"I have strength for all things in Christ Who empowers me I am ready for anything and equal to anything through Him Who infuses inner strength into me; I am self-sufficient in Christ's sufficiency]."
Philippians 4:13 AMPC

"For My thoughts are not your thoughts, neither are your ways My ways, says the Lord. For as the heavens are higher than the earth, so are My ways higher than your ways and My thoughts than your thoughts."

Isaiah 55:8-9 AMPC

"Do not let your hearts be troubled (distressed, agitated). You believe in and adhere to and trust in and rely on God; believe in and adhere to and trust in and rely also on Me. In my Father's house there are many dwelling places(homes). If it were not so, I would have told you; for I am going away to prepare a place for you. And when I go and make ready a place for you, I will come back again and will take you to Myself, that where I am you may be also. And to the place where I am going you know the way."

John 14:1-4 AMPC

"Call to Me and I will answer you and show you great and mighty things, fenced in and hidden, which you do not know (do not distinguish and recognize, have knowledge of and understanding."
Jeremiah 33:3 AMPC

"We throw open our doors to God and discover at the same time He has already thrown open His doors to us. We find ourselves standing where we always hoped we might stand out in the wide-open spaces of God's grace and glory standing tall and shouting our praise."

Romans 5:1-2 The Message

"For thus says the Lord to the men of Judah and to Jerusalem: Break up your ground left uncultivated for a season, so that you may not sow among thorns."

Jeremiah 4:3 AMPC

_____
_____
_____
_____
_____
_____
_____
_____
_____
_____
_____
_____
_____
_____
_____
_____
_____
_____
_____
_____
_____
_____
_____
_____
_____
_____

"You will show me the path of life; in Your presence is fullness of joy, at Your right hand there are pleasures forevermore."

Psalm 16:11 AMPC

"Write this. Write what you see. Write it out in big block letters so that it can be read on the run. This vision-message is a witness pointing to what's coming. It aches for the coming—it can hardly wait! And it doesn't lie. If it seems slow in coming, wait. It's on its way. It will come right on time."

Habakkuk 2:3-5 MSG

"Then said the Lord to me, 'You have seen well, for I am alert and active, watching over My word to perform it.'"

Jeremiah 1:12 AMPC

"Then he broke through and transformed all my wailing
into a whirling dance of ecstatic praise!
He has torn the veil and lifted from me
the sad heaviness of mourning.
He wrapped me in the glory garments of gladness.

How could I be silent when it's time to praise you?
Now my heart sings out loud, bursting with joy—
a bliss inside that keeps me singing,
I can never thank you enough!"

Psalm 30:11 TPT

*"You did it: you changed wild lament into whirling dance;
You ripped off my black mourning band and
decked me with wildflowers."*

Psalm 30:11 MSG

_____
_____
_____
_____
_____
_____
_____
_____
_____
_____
_____
_____
_____
_____
_____
_____
_____
_____
_____
_____
_____
_____
_____

> *"The Lord God is my Strength, my personal bravery, and my invincible army; He makes my feet like hinds' feet and will make me to walk [not to stand still in terror, but to walk] and make [spiritual] progress upon my high places [of trouble, suffering, or responsibility]!"*
>
> Habakkuk 3:19 AMPC

_____
_____
_____
_____
_____
_____
_____
_____
_____
_____
_____
_____
_____
_____
_____
_____
_____
_____
_____
_____
_____
_____

> "You've gone into my future to prepare the way, and in kindness you follow behind me to spare me from the harm of my past."
>
> Psalms 139:5 TPT

"His comfort rings loud and clear in. Do not earnestly remember the former things; neither consider the things of old. Behold, I am doing a new thing! Now it springs forth; do you not perceive and know it and will you not give heed to it? I will even make a way in the wilderness and rivers in the desert."

Isaiah 43:18-AMPC

_____
_____
_____
_____
_____
_____
_____
_____
_____
_____
_____
_____
_____
_____
_____
_____
_____
_____
_____
_____
_____
_____

"It's impossible to disappear from you or to ask the darkness to hide me, or to ask the darkness to hide me, for your presence is everywhere, bringing light into my night."

Psalm 139:11 TPT

_____
_____
_____
_____
_____
_____
_____
_____
_____
_____
_____
_____
_____
_____
_____
_____
_____
_____
_____
_____
_____
_____
_____
_____

> "This resurrection life you received from God is not a timid, grave-tending life. It's adventurously expectant, greeting God with a childlike 'What's next, Papa?' God's Spirit touches our spirits and confirms who we really are. We know who he is, and we know who we are: Father and children. And we know we are going to get what's coming to us—an unbelievable inheritance! We go through exactly what Christ goes through. If we go through the hard times with him, then we're certainly going to go through the good times with him!"
>
> Romans 8:15-17 The Message

Made in the USA
Middletown, DE
14 March 2022